DATE DUE

THE ESKIMOS KNEW

THE Eskimos

WHITTLESEY HOUSE

Knew

by **TILLIE S. PINE**
and **JOSEPH LEVINE**

Illustrated by Ezra Jack Keats

McGraw-Hill Book Company, Inc.   New York   Toronto   London

Also by Tillie S. Pine and Joseph Levine

with pictures by Ezra Jack Keats

THE INDIANS KNEW

THE PILGRIMS KNEW

THE CHINESE KNEW

with pictures by Bernice Myers

AIR ALL AROUND

FRICTION ALL AROUND

LIGHT ALL AROUND

SOUNDS ALL AROUND

WATER ALL AROUND

with pictures by Anne Marie Jauss

MAGNETS AND HOW TO USE THEM

18001

THE ESKIMOS KNEW

Copyright © 1962 by Tillie S. Pine, Joseph Levine, and Ezra Jack Keats. Printed in the United States of America. All rights reserved. This book or parts thereof may not be reproduced in any form without the permission of the publishers.

LIBRARY OF CONGRESS CATALOG CARD NUMBER: 61:17945

Published by Whittlesey House, a division of the McGraw-Hill Book Company, Inc.

Third Printing

Did you ever wonder
why the people of the cold lands
of the North are called
     ESKIMOS?

     There is a story that long, long ago
the Indians who lived in the land south
of where the Eskimos lived gave them
this name.   It means
     "Raw-meat-eaters."

     In this book you will read
about the Eskimos of long ago
and you will find out about many things
they knew and did.
     You will see how they used
the ice, the snow, the animals around them.
     You will do some experiments that
will help you understand
how the Eskimos were able to live
in this cold, cold part of our earth.

The Eskimos knew

that they could get fresh water
from salty sea water.
While hunting and fishing on the frozen sea,
they looked for large blocks of ice
that were bluish in color.
This was the sea water
that had frozen the year before.
During the short summer time
the ice melted a little at a time.
But, each time it melted,
the ice soon froze again.
While the ice blocks were melting and freezing,
melting and freezing,
the salt slowly worked its way out.
The Eskimos melted some of this bluish ice
and had fresh water for drinking.

Today

we, too, get fresh water
from salty sea water.
We are building large factories in which
different kinds of machines are used
to take the salt out of the sea water.
This is done by freezing the sea water,
or by boiling the sea water, or by using chemicals.

You

can get fresh water from salty water.
You will use heat to help you.
Put three tablespoons of salt
into a clean saucepan half full of water.
Stir the mixture until the salt dissolves.
Taste the water. Salty, isn't it?
Put a dry cover on the saucepan
and boil the salt water.
After a few minutes, take off the cover
and put it on the table, upside down.
You see water on the cover.
Let the cover cool off.
Taste the water on the cover.
It is fresh water!
When the water in the saucepan cools,
taste it. It is still salty.
The water that boils off from the salty water
is fresh—
because the salt stays in the saucepan water.

The Eskimos knew

how to protect their eyes
from the strong glare of light.
They invented snow goggles!
They carved these goggles out of bone
or driftwood and made
narrow slits in them.
The slits let only a small amount
of the glaring light shine through.
They wore these goggles
when they were outdoors
to protect their eyes
from the strong reflection of light
on the snow and ice.

Today

we put colored glass in our sun glasses.
This glass lets only small amounts of light
go through. We use these sun glasses
to protect our eyes—
> when we are at the beach,
> when we go skiing,
> when we drive cars.

You

can make your own toy "goggles."
Cut two narrow slits for your eyes
in a strip of cardboard.
Tie a piece of string
or elastic to the ends
of the cardboard.
Wear your "goggles" outdoors in the sunlight.

The Eskimos knew

that smooth things slide more easily
than rough things do.
They covered the runners of their sleds
with mud and let the mud freeze.
Then they poured water over the frozen mud.
The water froze and became ice.
They rubbed the rough ice smooth.
The smooth runners helped the sleds
slide easily and quickly
when the dogs pulled them
over the snow and ice.

Today

we, too, make things smooth
when we want them to slide
easily and quickly.
We put smooth steel runners on sleds.
We rub wax on smooth skis
to make them smoother.

You

can prove that things that are smooth
slide more easily than things that are rough.
Tack a piece of sandpaper to the bottom
of an empty covered cigar box.
This is now the rough side of the box.
Push the box, rough side down,
across an old table cloth.
Now push the box, smooth top down,
across the cloth.
On which side does the box slide more easily?

The Eskimos knew

how to build waterproof boats.
They made frames of walrus bone,
whalebone, or driftwood.
They sewed sealskins together
and covered the frames with them.
The sealskins were waterproof.
The Eskimos made small boats
called *kayaks* for one man to row.
They also made large boats called *umiaks*
that could hold many Eskimos.

Today

we build boats and ships
of many different kinds
of waterproof materials.
We use steel, plastic, fiber glass,
aluminum, and special kinds of wood.

You

can make your own toy waterproof boat.
Build a simple frame
in the shape of a boat.
Use thin strips of wood
or wire to do this.
Cover the outside of your frame with a single piece
of aluminum foil.
Have fun sailing your boat
in a tub of water.

The Eskimos knew

how to use air to keep things floating.
They sewed up large sealskin bags.
They blew them up like balloons
and tied them to their harpoon lines.
The Eskimo fishermen
threw their harpoons into a whale.
The large sealskin floats made it harder
for the harpooned whale
to dive down deep in the water to escape.
This tired the whale.
In this way, the air floats
helped the Eskimos capture the whale.

Today

we use cork, light woods,
and rubber to make floats.
We make water wings, life preservers, and life rafts
and fill them with air.
These are floats.
We even use floats called pontoons
on sea planes.

You

can see how air floats can keep
a heavy thing from sinking.
Remove the cover of an empty cigar box.
Float the box in a tub of water.
Put a few heavy stones into the box,
one at a time.   What happens?
The box soon sinks to the bottom.
Now—take the box and stones
out of the water.
Attach two blown-up balloons to the box,
one on each side.
Put the box into the water.
Put the stones back into the box.
What happens now?   The box does *not* sink.
Your air floats keep it floating!

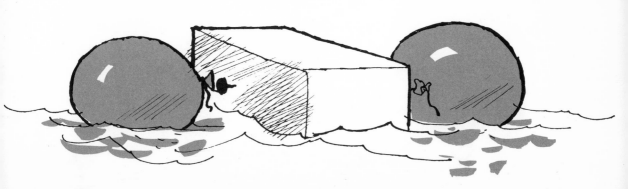

The Eskimos knew
how to find direction.
They did not have compasses to help them.
They saw that the wind blew the snow
into rows of snow mounds.
When they went hunting
they followed these rows
or they crossed them
to help them find their way.

Today

we, too, know how to find direction.
But—
we have compasses.
We use them on ships,
on planes, and in submarines
to help us find direction.

You

can find direction
and—you can make your own compass
to help you.
Rub a steel sewing needle
on one end of a magnet
about twenty times.   Make sure
that you rub the needle one way only.
Put a flat piece of cork
into a dish of water.
Lay the magnetized needle on the cork.
When the cork stops turning
the needle will point north and south.
Ask Father to tell you which end
of the needle is pointing north.
Now you can use your compass
to help you find North, South, East, West—
inside or outside your house.

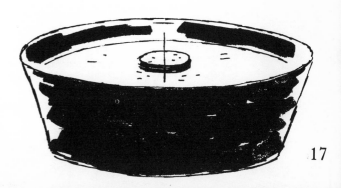

The Eskimos knew

how to use snow to protect themselves.
They cut blocks of hard snow and put them together
to make their round-shaped houses.
They filled the cracks
between the snow blocks with loose snow.
They called their houses "igloos."
Their igloos kept them safe and warm.
The Eskimos who lived in the far North
lived in their snow houses all year round.
Other Eskimos built them only during the winter
on their hunting or fishing trips.

Today

we use many different kinds of materials
to build our houses to protect ourselves.
We use bricks, wood, stone, steel,
aluminum, and glass.
We make our houses
of many different sizes and shapes.

You

can have fun
building a small snow house,
if you have snow where you live.
You can make large snowballs
and use them to make your snow house.
You can use a large cardboard for the roof
of your snow house.
The picture shows you how.

The Eskimos knew

that light can go through some things.
They used these things to make their windows.
They cut a thin piece
from a large block of ice.   They set
this thin piece of ice into an open space
in the wall of their igloo.
Sometimes they used
the insides of seals, called seal-gut,
in this space.
This was the "window" of the igloo.
The sunlight and the moonlight
shone through the window, into the igloo.

Today

we, too, know that light goes
through some things.
We use glass in our windows.
We sometimes use glass bricks and plastics
in walls and roofs to let more light
into our homes and factories.

You

can do something to show that
light goes through some things.
Cut a peephole in one end
of a covered shoe box.
Cut a "window" in the other end.
Cover the window with a piece of wax paper.
Look through the peephole.
You see light coming through the wax paper.
Now cover the window in turn with a cardboard,
a glass plate, a piece of cloth, a piece of paper.
Do you see light coming through any of these things?
You found out that light goes through
some things and does not go through
other things.

The Eskimos knew

how to keep heat inside their snow igloos.
They covered the inside walls
of their igloos with animal skins.
The skins kept the heat from going through the walls.
We say the Eskimos "insulated" their houses.

Today

we, too, insulate houses.
We use many different kinds of materials.
We use asbestos, rock wool,
fiber glass, aluminum, or paper
in walls and ceilings.

You

can see how insulation helps
to keep heat in.
Next time Mother bakes potatoes,
ask her to let you try an experiment.
When the potatoes are taken out of the oven, try this.
Wrap one hot baked potato in a towel.
Leave another hot baked potato unwrapped.
About ten minutes later,
uncover the wrapped potato.
Feel both potatoes. Which feels warmer?
The one that was wrapped
in the towel does. The towel
"insulated" the potato.
It kept the heat in the potato.

The Eskimos knew

that burning oil gives light and heat.
They invented a new kind of lamp.
They made a bowl
out of a piece of stone.
They made a wick
out of dried grass.
They put seal or walrus fat,
called "blubber," into this bowl.
They lighted the wick.
The blubber melted into oil.
The oil soaked into the wick—
and was burned.
The Eskimos used this oil lamp
to give them light and heat.

Today

people in many parts of the world
burn oil in lamps for lighting.
They also burn oil in furnaces
for heating.

You

can make your own oil-burning "lamp."
Ask your mother to help you.
Pour some cooking oil
into a small empty orange-juice can.
Stand this can in a larger can, in the sink.
You use the sink because it is safe to work there.
Stand a piece of stiff cord,
five inches long, in the oil.
Watch how the cord soaks up the oil.
Now light the dry top end of the cord.
(Be careful not to touch the hot can.)
See how brightly your oil lamp burns.
Put out your oil lamp by covering it
with a metal cover.
Do not touch the lamp until it has cooled.

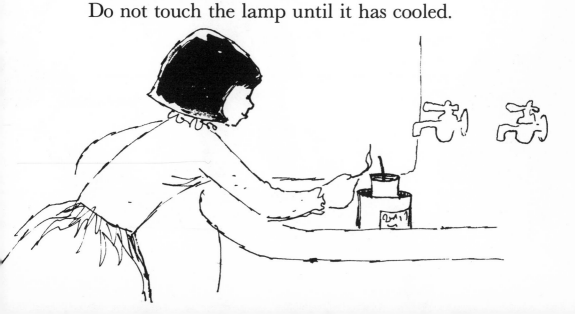

25

The Eskimos knew

that they could keep food from spoiling
by freezing it.
They let their raw meat and fish freeze.
They stored this frozen food
in storerooms built of ice and snow.
When the Eskimos were ready to eat,
they brought the frozen food
into their warm igloos.
The food thawed out.
The Eskimos ate their food raw.

Today

we freeze many different kinds
of cooked and uncooked foods to keep them from spoiling.
We freeze food in large freezers in factories
and in small freezers in our homes.

You

can prove that freezing food will keep it
from spoiling.
Wrap a small piece of raw meat
in wax paper. Put it in the freezing part
of your refrigerator.
Wrap another piece of raw meat, the same size,
in another piece of wax paper.
Put this one in an open jar on a shelf.
A few days later, take out the frozen piece of meat.
Let it thaw out.
Unwrap both pieces of meat. *Smell* each piece.
The piece that was on the shelf
smells spoiled. The frozen piece
smells fresh.

The Eskimos knew

how to soften animal skins.
They scraped the under part of the fur
and let it dry.
They did this again and again.
Sometimes the Eskimo women chewed the skins
with their strong teeth.
The scraping, the drying, the chewing—
all loosened the strong fibers in the skins,
and helped make the skins soft.
The Eskimos used these soft skins
to make clothing for their families.
They even made soft little leather boots
for their sled dogs.

Today

we, too, soften animal skins.
Furriers scrape, soak,
and dry skins to get the furs soft.
They call this "dressing" the skins.
Then they sew them together to make
coats, hats, scarves, muffs and gloves.

You

will not soften animal skins
because it is too difficult to do.
But—
ask Mother to take you
to a furrier's shop.
Ask him to show you
the different kinds of furs
in his shop.   You may even see
how he sews the "dressed" skins together.

FURS

29

The Eskimos knew

that wood can soak up water.
They saved the tiny pieces of cuttings
when they carved wood.
They rubbed these wood shavings on their skins
when they wanted to dry themselves.
The wood shavings were their towels.

Today

we, too, know that wood can soak up water.
Some storekeepers use sawdust
to dry off wet floors.
We also use towels of linen, cotton,
and paper for drying.

You

can see that wood can soak up water.
Ask your butcher to give you some sawdust.
Put the sawdust in a tray and add a little water.
See how the sawdust soaks up the water.
Add more water, a little at a time.
Are you surprised to see how much water
the sawdust can soak up?

Eskimos still live in the far North.

And—

some Eskimos live in Alaska,
our forty-ninth state.

Many Eskimos still do the things
you read about in this book.

But—

many Eskimos have changed their way of living
in their homeland.

They cook their food.

They live in modern houses.

They wear modern clothing.

They even travel in automobiles
and airplanes!